More Praise

"Reading Victor Clevenger is like stepping into a pair of well-worn, but still comfortable shoes; they might not be what's in fashion, but they'll take you where you need to be. His poems are snapshots into the hearts of the lives of us all. With great tenderness, but also (sometimes ruthlessly) without apology, *Corned Beef Hash by Candlelight* is Clevenger at his finest, truest, and most devastatingly real. Not only will you find all the hallmarks that make Clevenger Clevenger, in this book you will also find this everyman's poet treading new ground with the epic whirlwind that is excerpt from The Foxes. You will also be treated to a second chance at the phenomenal reggie poems originally found in *On the Tips of Our Tongues*. *Corned Beef Hash by Candlelight* is not for ones with a weak constitution, but is a must for anyone interested in seeing the sublime light to be found in the cracks of our dark world."

- James Benger
author of *The Park*
(Aldrich Press, 2019)

With tough guy bravery, heart that will sweeten your brew, and uninhibited sexiness, *Corned Beef Hash by Candlelight* is a full entree of poetry. The unpredictability of life shifts from something lonely to something beautiful with the additions of friends, children, and lovers. This collection is founded on the wisdom that we each carry the sunlight of hope.

-Linzi Garcia
Author of *Thank You*
(Spartan Press, 2018)

For Brandon,
The excitement of evolution—
It's a rough kind of beautiful.
Thanks for grabbing up a copy.
Cheers!
— Victor

Corned Beef Hash by Candlelight

Poems by Victor Clevenger

7/15/19

#021

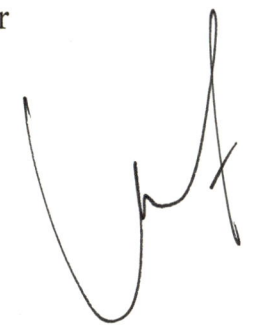

Luchador Press
Big Tuna, TX

Copyright © Victor Clevenger, 2019
First Edition 1 3 5 7 9 10 8 6 4 2
ISBN: 978-1-950380-41-1
LCCN: 2019943085

Design, edits and layout: El Dopa
Interior images: Victor Clevenger
Author photo: Victor Clevenger
All rights reserved. No part of this publication may be reproduced or transmitted in any form or by any means, electronic or mechanical, including photocopying, recording or by info retrieval system, without prior written permission from the author.

Acknowledgments:

Grateful acknowledgement is given to the editors at *The Gasconade Review, Rose of Sharon Press, Blue Hour, Least Bittern Books, Ramingo's Porch, Apache Poetry Blog, Misfit Magazine, Trailer Park Quarterly, Ted Ate America 5, 365 Poems Anthology, Horror Sleaze Trash, San Pedro River Review, The Dope Fiend Daily, Holy&intoxicated Publications* and *Thimble Lit Magazine* where some of these pieces have previously appeared.

The poems from the chapbook *On The Tip Of Our Tongues* were originally published in a limited press run of 25 copies by Analog Submission Press in 2018.

TABLE OF CONTENTS

Foreward by Jason Baldinger

Christian Ready for the Fire / 1

Mother's Day Mayhem / 3

Our Living / 4

Downtime in Iraq / 5

Behind Battle Lines & Bars / 6

Sharing the Ghosts of Yesterdays / 7

A Poem Written after Pulling Memoirs
   of a Street Poet off the Shelf on the Night
   That I Heard Frankie Died / 8

Sleeping With My Muse / 9

Looking Through a Telescope / 10

Jelly Jar / 11

In This Room / 12

Poem for Blake McIntyre / 13

The Army Has Invaded: Poem #1 / 16

The Army Has Invaded: Poem #2 / 17

The Army Has Invaded: Poem #3 / 18

The Army Has Invaded: Poem #4 / 19

The Army Has Invaded: Poem #5 / 20

Nobody Wants This Stink / 21

Ghosts on Crouch St. / 22

Birthday Séance Haiku / 23

Thirty Years / 24

Off the Ledge like a Bird / 26

Hush Kitty / 28

A Horse He Called Beautiful / 29

My Mannequin at Barb's Books / 31

Pants at Easter / 32

One of Three Sides to a Story / 34

Desire is a Box Built from Cherry Wood & Poplar / 35

Beautiful Things Attract Beautiful Things / 36

Peace Lilies / 37

Found Poem: Woody's 50's Diner / 38

You Can't Escape What You Can't Escape / 39

Cold Love Poem / 42

Wide-Eyed Wild / 43

Five Degrees in January / 44

Tonight Like a Jukebox / 45

In the Heat of a Moment / 46

Jealousy is a Dirty Windshield / 47

Corned Beef Hash by Candlelight / 48

Pine Scent & Marijuana / 49

A Black Snake Moaning Under a Shining Moon / 50

Sharing a Shower / 51

Like a Naked Woman in Sunshine / 52

Melting Roads / 54

From Father's Day to the First Frost / 56

Humming Champagne Supernova / 57

Morning's Hungover / 58

Bones Age with Each Breath / 59

Insanity / 61

Cold Rain Blues / 62

Silent in Love / 63

Trying to Hold a Heart Hostage / 64

Sweet Chili Sauce on Cold Days When the Sun
  Stayed Asleep Until Noon / 65

Strawberry Body Milk Poem / 66

Days on Lathrop St. / 67

Sucking Blues Away / 68

Shoelaces / 69

excerpt from The Foxes / 72

An Acquired Taste / 78

I See You in Cities: Poem #1 / 80

I See You in Cities: Poem #2 / 81

Two Haiku / 82

Four to Six / 83

Cheeking Haldol / 84

Pearl / 85

Poem for Jameson Bayles / 86

Poem for Kyra at 2 A.M. / 87

With Ten Toes & an Extra Heartbeat inside You / 88

Four Flights to Freedom / 89

Meth Rock in His Pocket / 90

On The Tip Of Our Tongues / 93

My Best Friend / 97

Graveyard Shift / 98

On a Thursday / 100

Reggie's Advice During My 1st Marriage / 102

Continued Quest for a John Dorsey Book / 103

Reunion / 104

Forced Sober / 105

Kiss & Tell / 107

That Taste on the Tip of Our Tongues / 108

Hot Action & Appreciation / 110

What Am I Going To Do With My Life / 112

Nuclear Goodbyes / 113

Traveler / 115

FOREWORD

A friend recently said to me, in our lifetimes they're gonna find out the time moves both backwards and forwards. Sure, we we're heavy with drink and cosmic substances but that doesn't matter too damn much, what matters is it might be true. I mean we have conceptualized time, capitalism put a price on it and we process it mostly incorrectly. Really, for all the talk no one knows, and that's where poets are invaluable.

I was in Blue Springs, Missouri, in October 2016, it was the last night of a tour. I had raced through cities like Columbus, Indianapolis, Detroit, and Chicago. I found the part of Iowa they keep like a secret, the part that unfolds in rolling hills, the part that unfolds under the sun the same way a woman does naked under the sheets. I had seen a sunset in Lawrence, Kansas, that still makes me cry. I had rested my head on Charlie Parker's tombstone and felt that I understood home in some even more broken way. Now, here I am in some dusty Wild West town that has boiled hot dogs for happy hour.

There's a bookstore in town that's hosting this batch of rowdies, almost all deeply settled into middle age. A Pittsburgh contingent meeting with a Kansas and Missouri contingent. A summit if you will, where all the similar experiences of being and losing get unpacked in fifteen minutes each on stage.

We had already had the bonding experience of being hassled by the cops, because this ain't the Wild West anymore, it's the Midwest. I mean what the fuck are all these ne're-do-well poets think they're doing wandering through town like they own hope. Hope was fucking outlawed when they hung the last horse, that spot is now a fast food joint that serves a passable milkshake.

Anyway, there were a lot of moments that night, eight poets all armed to the teeth tackling the stage, no one out of rhythm, no one missed. Goddamn all these crazy writer poets on fire and realizing they went to different schools together. For a second we are not all alone in the universe. Goddamn it, fair readers it was a beautiful thing.

That was the first night I met Victor Adam Clevenger.

Now you see Victor is a quiet cat. He's always watching and reading. He's the same kind of poet, quiet as a summer breeze, but those words get on you and it brings the same relief, the same revelation. You know it's hard to write poems about an army of ants and a poem about morning sex and give them equal weight. That's Victor, equal weight, a shining moment like every moment, incandescent on the page.

Over the years we've talked about editing in New Orleans knock-off bars lost in Kansas City. We've been eulogized by drunks sitting at a round table filled with fried chicken in Belle, Missouri. We've kissed the same ex-stripper under a full moon outside my crooked house in Pittsburgh. We've marveled at the thousand poems you can write to a Salina sky. We've stood at confluence of three river and fell in love with a universe we will never understand. We've crushed quite a few can of High Life and shared stories of life on the road, a life completely ordinary but somehow completely unstuck in time.

Here we are now out of time and at the end of a foreword and you have Corned Beef Hash by Candlelight to read like a picnic lunch at Everette Maddox's tombstone. The sound in your right ear may be Ted Berrigan whispering, and there's a diner in Weatherford, Oklahoma, that's just another lost lonely lover. There's only one case of champagne pony bottles left in the world and everything fragile is broken. If I didn't know any better I'd tell you this is the last best place on earth.

Now read on lumberjack!

—Jason Baldinger

for Jason Ryberg

The Excitement of Evolution

Christian Ready for the Fire

with his hair parted
slicked to the right like mine
he orders the kung pow chicken
drizzles sriracha for good measure
then forks a bite

that afternoon at the china restaurant
on old highway 24
i watch my son push through the pain
just to be like his old man

on the drive home
i tell him just wait
because the feeling isn't over

he says   ugh
i know
all things that enter
must pass through

you're right   i reassure him

each morning
you'll sit on the cold seat
reflecting on decisions you've made

& some won't feel good

but you'll wipe your ass clean
stand up
wash your hands
look in the mirror
& consider yourself lucky

to still be producing
& breathing the stink

because you're alive

& understand
that the dead

can no longer do

what you

can do

Mother's Day Mayhem

some nights
call for a few beers
& shots of rum come breakfast time
it's those same kind of nights
when i think about you
more than myself
you sitting at home
swallowing coffee & worry
me standing
in intense silence
under a moon that has one eye closed
with uncertainty
we both listen & wait
for the madhouse
to exhale its final breath
& be gone
this morning
i told you
that if broken glass could be melted into hope
i had walked over enough last night to know
that things are going to be okay
but that's fantasy
& as we laughed together
you passed the bacon
i tipped the bottle

Our Living

poor

was pain
to you & i

but when the
children were

young

they were
none the
wiser

& that was
a success we
accomplished
together

Downtime in Iraq

i heard stories
that the madman had
the most beautiful creatures
living somewhere within those waters
so every other day before breakfast
i would tie a string to a tree
throw sweet bagels attached to fishing hooks
into the death-pool-drainage lake
that trickled slowly
like lanced lesions from
the spread wide thighs
of the mighty tigris
after weeks waiting
i finally hooked the jawbone of something beautiful
struggled with its resistance
but eventually gained surrender
holding it in my homesick hands
i almost felt the urge to cry
i remember telling myself
don't do it   &   toughen up
who cries during wars anyway
with the urge growing stronger
i released the fish   &
stared straight into the sun without glasses
just to have an excuse
i wasn't tough enough to hold back tears
but i found ways around it
we all did   & i'm sure
we all still do

Behind Battle Lines & Bars
for matt borczon

swallowing hard
to the slow tick of a clock
the sky gets dark
when ghosts wrap thin films
of yesterdays
around your eyes
a reminder that
the greatest war
a man will wage
will not be
against his enemies
it will be against himself
the human mind
will always be a battlefield
filled with images
of hell
you learn
the trick is
to lift the sun by strings
tied to your footsteps
while running forward with hope
towards the radio transmissions
of a better tomorrow

Sharing the Ghosts of Yesterdays

nosediving deep into the depths
of a warm reassurance
saying
you once had slipped
from great heights
& got stuck in a moment

where your side was ripped open
by a crooked nail

& at first the blood ran down softly
like the tone of a whisper
but it built up quickly
to an intoxicating level of fear

that more demons would be summoned
than angels

to help sing the chorus

of just another sad swan song about falling
from the heavens

too many times

to walk away without scars

A Poem Written after Pulling Memoirs of
a Street Poet off the Shelf on the Night That I
Heard Frankie Died

grasping heartbeats
through skin
&
holding firm
like trapping a bee

between cupped hands
& breasts

intrigued

by how it feels

harmless

Sleeping With My Muse

like every frank t. rios
page set ablaze
i want you to wake me
from my dreams
on fire
all hours of the day
i want you to dance like
smoke through my skin layers
as i grasp to hold you in
i want you to stain
my fingertips permanent
like how ink bleeds
into the fibers of paper
i want you to leave your mark
on me
leave me no doubts
that you
       are the reason
we burn

Looking Through a Telescope
for mick guffan

craters in the surface of the moon

deep enough to hide
the secrets of our existence in

deep enough to hide
a thousand handfuls of pills in

i wonder

how many secrets
& how many pills would get swallowed

on lonely nights

before your black sky turned tangerine

Jelly Jar

i remember her walking
across cold wooden floorboards
towards a kitchen sink
where a jelly jar sat half-full of water

she only stopped long enough
to take a sip
but as she sat it back down   unleveled
it fell & shattered into pieces

holding her hand up
as if to say   nobody move
she started singing a patsy cline song
as she swept broken pieces of glass
into an old dustpan

this was the first time
that i'd heard her sing a sad song
but as i grew older & heard the stories
of the sudden shoves down stairs
the heartache   & her black-eye nights

it made sense to me
as to why this first time
wasn't the last time

In This Room

in the middle of the afternoon from a great distance
the sun is only a few inches wide
it's small

sitting on the ledge
near a window that we call cold
is a dying cactus

dirt dry & dreaming of better days

you say   it's like standing over a deathbed
we have to show it that we care
& the best thing that we can probably do
is to touch it

give it a real good loving embrace with our fingers
& our palms

but we can't shout

to make this all seem sincere

we just have to take the pain—

don't we

Poem for Blake McIntyre

long after the chalked hash marks
have washed away
with all the youthful dreams
of superstardom

& the friday night lights
have been shut out early enough
to catch just enough shuteye
to make it through another weekend shift
at the job

trying to earn enough money
to make ends meet in these depressed days
is no easy feat

you tell everyone
that will listen
to trust you

that the responsibility of adulthood

is no pancake platter at jerry's diner

The Army Has Invaded: Poem #1

sound the trumpets   ring the bells
in step a whole platoon curves around a peach pit
half-smoked joint lying in an ashtray
another day another ant parade
sweetly stoned & graceful
how long you plan on staying
i ask without receiving a reply
i learn   they don't give two-shits about me

The Army Has Invaded: Poem #2

march along march strong
marching soldiers march
nine black ants making their way up the side
of a cup
two days old
they won't listen   spoiled milk mission
it's not going to be sweet
march along march strong
marching soldiers march
i turn the kitchen light out & say   good luck
imagining their wives waiting at home
holding tiny heart-shaped lockets in their hands

The Army Has Invaded: Poem #3

i tell one of the ants that has strayed away
that he is probably safe
that he's far too small to have to worry
about someone
shooting him with a bullet
i wish i could say the same to my children
monday thru friday
when i give them their lunch money

The Army Has Invaded: Poem #4

cleaning up dried kool-aid by the coffee pot
graceyn says these ants are brave
or stupid   & i agree with her
either way you look at it though
the army is two-hundred strong tonight
clinging to a toaster they've turned into a foxhole
taking turns sleeping
with sugared mandibles
& pride
we thought about looking for the queen
but didn't really know what was appropriate to do
if we found her

The Army Has Invaded: Poem #5

it's ferlinghetti's birthday &
the youth of a nation shout in the streets
nobody should have to worry while falling asleep
but i wake with the soldiers
crawling on the lens of my eyeglasses
picking them up off the nightstand
i use my finger to swat them away
& i'm sure they'll come back
another day   because of course
they're trained for the war
so it's far more enjoyable than the peace
i want you all gone goddammit   i tell them
just go home to your wives tonight
& make love
so tomorrow when the sun rises
we can all smile about our victories

Nobody Wants This Stink

forced down the throat
of a toilet bowl
yesterday
my morning shit
was peachy orange
not a bright peach
not a bright orange
a burnt color smeared on paper
the porcelain refused
to swallow it voluntarily
i felt guilty
walking back into the room
with a plunger
in my hand
like i worked for
fox news

Ghosts on Crouch St.

death blows
down my street
from the south

making scratching sounds
against the asphalt

i wonder how long
these naked trees
will grieve
their children

lying
in the cracks
against the curbs
again

Birthday Séance Haiku

somewhere ghosts of good men
lick their sweet lips
as john dorsey eats his pie

Thirty Years

one small foot leads the other in a race
across childhood memories slowly
a growing shadow casts around a corner
looking like a crooked smile
familiar
gathered honeybees on the front porch screen
makes a buzzing sound
like hair clippers gliding through summer's growth
she squeezes wooden clothespins
between the thumb & fingers
whistles the best that she can
when she's done
the lines sag under the weight
let's go
climb in
make room
the devil went down to georgia
his favorite song on the radio
dashboard gauges useless   malfunctioned
but not a worry
a '79 thunderbird with the windows cracked
going to grandma's place
we were cruising at a speed of simplicity
that will never be felt again
that was thirty years ago

i light another cigarette
turn on don lemon   tonight
i am aging in a world of madness
falling apart
& all of my fears are the glue sticking the skin
to these bones
i am an arts-n-crafts project
from room to room
kissing my children goodnight
i wonder what
they will remember thirty years from now
on a thursday
in the month of april
when the sun slides out of the sky
& they're sitting all alone
at their kitchen tables

Off the Ledge like a Bird

at some point you must simply just leap
flames rising burning
rain falling drowning
wind blowing scattering
cold creeping freezing
dog dying elderly
kids crying argumentative
work daily draining
sun falling darkness
naked woman beautiful
loving woman distant
whiskey tonic drinking
eyes closing intoxication
alarm clock shouting
morning stomach nauseating
nauseating morning stomach
shouting alarm clock
intoxication eyes closing
drinking whiskey tonic
distant loving women
beautiful naked women
darkness falling sun
draining work daily
argumentative kids crying
elderly dog dying

freezing cold creeping
scattering wind blowing
drowning rain falling
burning flames rising
just leap at some point you must simply

Hush Kitty

eyes glow
staring out
from behind a curtain

as if to remind me
that she knows
all my dirty secrets

i call her over
to a food bowl
& give her anything she wants

because i know
that she definitely does not know
all my secrets

but i know
that she knows

more than most

A Horse He Called Beautiful

when all the rest would sleep
we would sit & i'd listen to stories
she'd laugh her way through some
grind her teeth with disgust during others
& look at the floor
when one of them shook loose a sad memory

i remember a story that she said was some
. . . . amazing disappearing acts & shit

said once it was bedtime
her husband would pull the sheets over himself
wait until she'd fallen asleep
& then vanish until the daylight came back again

said that in the late 40's
which would have been her early 20's
she spent a lot of time cussing the rooster's crow

knowing that she'd wake up lonely
& without the courage to set him straight
with the smack of her hand
against his dirty lying cheek

once he slipped back home over hills

half-sober sitting crooked in the saddle
on a long-legged horse

that she swore he loved far more than he loved her

My Mannequin at Barb's Books

we could have ruled the world together   she said

you made me feel a little less hollow inside

Pants at Easter

laughing at forgotten things
when remembered

wiping his hand across his knee   steve said
one time his pants were wrinkled

that's not very funny

he said   it gets better

lit a fire under a street lamp to smoke out bugs
hovering in the shouts of a hectic night

tried to stomp it out
& caught the pants on fire
jumped around
kicked off shoes
ripped away the pants
limped a few yards down the sidewalk
walked hunchbacked
looking at his bare legs
said the bugs were most likely laughing

his girlfriend was furious

she'd bought the pants at easter time
from her sister who wanted twenty dollars
& a burgundy pair of foster grant glasses for them

she paid ten & a chicken sandwich
told me not to tear holes in the knees
doing stupid shit

& i promised her i wouldn't

he started laughing again   this time
at a spoon on a table

& said i got another story to tell you

about an ice cream sandwich in troy, ohio

& a picture of a turtle
that i drew last march

One of Three Sides to a Story

that man has kissed his last opportunity goodbye
there's no way in hell
that my sweet ass will ever take him back
bent over at the waist
the girl beside a crow that's pecking at the ground
could tell anyone her problems
but today she chooses birds

my grandmother liked birds
had houses in the yard for them
they were neighbors   a decent kind of crowd
that didn't make you uneasy
early morning eating toast
in front of an open window
when focused on distant things
like a golden sun stretching for half a block
up one side of a building & down the other

as the crow flies   she stops talking
& i wonder how the man she was referring to
feels about any of this

Desire is a Box Built from Cherry Wood & Poplar

i figured you were probably expecting something
a bit fancier than a heart like a rusty nail

i was wrong

Beautiful Things Attract Beautiful Things
for belle

a shimmer lingers

it shows me
you're not a stranger
to the dust of burning stars

if you were to tell me
you could catch a hot one
in the palm of your hands

& hold it
like a passionate heartbeat
keeping it warm until the sun rises

i'd believe you

Peace Lilies

for west, mississippi & john dorsey

it's an eerie feeling

seeing how blood runs down a wilted petal
& drips onto the crippled stem
that grows up through a claimed crack
in the concrete

hearts beating slowly like
a bullet nervously tapped against a pistol's barrel

pissing in the wind & praying

that even the ghosts
of the toughest outlaws which guide us

suggest retreat

Found Poem: Woody's 50's Diner

please………
whatever you do..
absolootly…
positively…..
do "not" look
into this hole

You Can't Escape What You Can't Escape

between sips of coffee
she tells me that it is not a bad job
fourteen dollars an hour with tips
& a meal mid-shift
but when she empties the ash trays
attached to the slot machines
the smell reminds her
of her mother's nightstand
when they lived in that hotel for a while
& even back then
she found it odd
that in the morning time
every man that her mother brought back
to have sex with
was introduced to her
as her uncle
like that was the solution
to make everything
that she had just experienced
seem better

Say a Prayer

Cold Love Poem

the key to prevent freezing
is to let love drip slowly

faucets attached to heart shaped pipes

i tell you

at six below zero in missouri
flesh is no more than a twin sheet
draped over bare bones

you agree

staring at the ceiling above us

we dream about crashing a car
into the sun

Wide-Eyed Wild

having sex on a couch once
like it was a cloud
inflated with some god's deep breath

she thought we were lovers dangling from the sun

asked if i could picture our shadows
stretched out for a thousand miles

asked if i thought it was odd
that our feet never seem to touch the rooftops
of this city that swallows us

i didn't think it was odd
    at all

just ran my fingertips through her hair
& let her talk beautiful to me

her lips parting were poems in themselves

words sharper than anything
cupid has ever pulled from
a quiver

& aimed in my direction

Five Degrees in January

steam covers the bathroom mirror

i kiss her in the shower

waiting on the moon to melt
our frozen city

Tonight Like a Jukebox

you're standing in the shower
singing joan jett
i hate myself for loving you

i'm alone in the next room
singing the divinyls
i touch myself

together we finish with
bad reputation

& neither of us give a damn

our shared secrets are the dimes
dropped into the coin slots
of tomorrow's crooked smiles

In the Heat of a Moment

an earring was a star

falling to the floor

&

i secretly wished

for a baby to grow inside her

Jealousy is a Dirty Windshield

while traveling these highways
in the frozen darkness

she is every falling star

that boys wish upon

Corned Beef Hash by Candlelight

on the hottest day yet

i slowly pulled my fingers
out from between her legs

the tips wet like paint brushes

that had been dipped
into every single color of love

she'd created

a skip in the beat of a heart

that evening we ate corned beef hash
by candlelight

& agreed
that if you squinted your eyes
while looking into the flame

you could see something beautiful

Pine Scent & Marijuana
for heather hamilton

our '97 life in a rear-view
day skies were green
night skies
were hot-kaleidoscope-orgasms

we said together we'd love forever
because a day without loving
would be a day of certain misery
that we would never choose to wake to

i've lived twenty-years of days since then
all ones we said we'd never choose

& i have no idea
if they are miserable for you
i only know that there are still dark mornings
when i can feel a warm vibration
of you whispering words
into my ear

i wake quickly
alone   & imagine

our aged bodies
dangling like slivers of driftwood
from two beaded nooses
in this dreamcatcher
above my headboard

A Black Snake Moaning Under a Shining Moon

love burning & chilling
distilling in a rib cage
drunken hearts make decisions
wake in the morning
devil's teeth clench
in reverence
alarm clock
killing us softly
long kiss
before goodbye
& a drive away

Sharing a Shower

she lathered her hair   scrubbed her skin
stepped to the back
i stepped into the water & did the same
rinsed first
reached down with my hands
grabbed my cheeks & spread them apart
leaned forward so that the water could rinse
my asshole clean
she laughed
i stopped rinsing & reached around her
grabbed her ass to spread her cheeks apart
then i laughed
she rinsed herself off
& we were done
afterwards
as we sat on the balcony
smoking   sharing red wine
i asked her
when she is at home tonight
with her husband & children
playing the role of fully committed
dinnertime discussing their afternoons
if i will cross her mind
when she says to them
that her day was uneventful
like any other day
these days

Like a Naked Woman in Sunshine

it's strange when the heat of the day
happens during the dark of the night
i'm always wide awake
lying there with my palm resting
between feminine thighs
wedged tight against the vagina of a woman
who intentionally sleeps with her body facing away
from me as i press yet another lonely hard-on
against her without success

i ask her in the morning as she wakes
did you hear the water dripping madly against the
windows

she never hears it
or admits to hearing it

she climbs out of the bed first & shivers
while she gets dressed

i lie there alone for a moment watching her tug
english rose stockings up above her knees   always
hopping on one foot & struggling with them

i soon climb out of the bed shivering too
& it is in this moment which i wonder
if other men at times have had these same kind
of nights like i have often had with her

sleepless & dreaming about someone else

Melting Roads

while navigating the ninth cloud
we shift through the gears
of the heart & the head

our secrets written on rusted street signs

we lose stability

slide sideways

into the sharp curves of a warm thirst

stopping at the driveway of desire
only to unlock the gate

Truth Is I'm Hooked on a Wicked Princess

From Father's Day to the First Frost

i believe in spirits
i cannot see

when two
voodoo dolls
are rubbed together

we both feel the tingle
in the flow of
our blood

Humming Champagne Supernova

the kids all sit oblivious in the kitchen
eating pancakes at the dinner table

we now in our late thirties
acting like 90's teens
sneaking down hallways

standing inside a bathroom during
a rainstorm

lightning outside
ripping through a cloud's bottoms
falling on trees like hot firework debris

crissy says   you better hurry up

as i pull my underwear down

like it was the first time with her
all over again

Morning's Hungover

too foolish
to accept that it could all be garbage

our love
will always be that pot of spaghetti
left out overnight on a stove

Bones Age with Each Breath

i wish i had an answer
wish i didn't have demons
didn't always feel like failing
i wish i didn't have a situation
was 22 again
i wish i was smarter
had gone to college
i wish i was living life
not letting life live me
i wish i had your heartbeat memorized
like a song by the national
wish i didn't feel everything closing
in on me   didn't always cry when i hurt
i wish that i could pick lilies for you
year round
walk to the kitchen right now
make you cinnamon rolls
i wish i was the earth to you
lick your armpits until you laugh
i wish i wasn't losing you to someone
that will never love you   i love you
i wish that my heart was actually an object
i could remove from my body
i would rip it out & give it to you without hesitation
as you sip your hot cup of vanilla biscotti

i light a cigarette
hazing the room like fog lifting over a cemetery
we've both seen
in a dream
but refuse to acknowledge

Insanity

flip an hour glass
 o   r   o
  v & e   v
    e   v & e
      r   o   r

grains drop like eyelids
ice floats in rum
      then melts
dirty sheets
from last night's sex
pulled up to your
waist
      is lonely
      it is what it is
      it is
another
sunday morning
missing
you

Cold Rain Blues

it's 3:20 in the afternoon
where are you with lips like springtime
tongue like summer

on the front steps of your house
i'm just another wet songbird full of desire

singing for you
without a reply

Silent in Love

we see
birds of prey circling
the spaces above
our heads

today

my heart is like a
starving lion

waiting for you to say anything
with nourishment

Trying to Hold a Heart Hostage

we'd ditch a backseat
for a seventy-nine dollar room
on the second floor

have sex with law & order
playing in the background

after all those times
listening to the secrets
of how the cops catch 'em

you would have thought
i'd been well-schooled

a hardened criminal

who knew not to rely solely
on the promise of
i love you

as a restraining
mechanism

Sweet Chili Sauce on Cold Days When the Sun Stayed Asleep Until Noon

the times of eating hot wings
on hotel sheets together
have passed

sucking on the bones
of those memories

our souls will never starve to death

Strawberry Body Milk Poem

in an unfamiliar room
my right hand & hard-on smell delicious

Days on Lathrop St.

it's like i have just
swallowed the
goddamn sun

& chased it down
with a shot of brandy

i don't love this feeling
but then again
i don't hate it either

it's just what my insides
feel like when you
are near me

Sucking Blues Away

after months passed
feeling love sick

she sat on the edge
of the kitchen sink

offering her nipple
like the tip of a needle

that contained
the cure

Shoelaces

one morning you'll wake up late   be in a rush to
get out the door to punch a time clock & find your
shoelaces tied together in many tight knots
you can't get undone

you'll shout & cuss me for doing such a thing
& i'll tell you that. it's. not. the end of the world

that it's just symbolism   that the laces are you & i
that the undone knots are our embraces

then i'll tell of how it took me hours thinking about
you & of a way to show you that you're important to me

my best guess is that you'll say   how the fuck does
tying my shoelaces into knots show importance

& i'll tell you that i guess you have to think
outside the box a bit

but in all honesty   you have always been
important to me   but if i've ever made you doubt that

i'm sorry

& that i'll untie the knots for you   but only if you promise to tie them back before you say goodbye

The Foxes

excerpt from The Foxes

the distance black & quiet   i'd fallen asleep on the
front porch when the rain turned into foxes
hanging from their neck were spoons & plates
i saw a thousand of them

a door underneath a flashing red sign would open &
they would all go inside   out of curiosity
people that were smoking pipes across the street
went inside too   all gathered in a very small space
they ate meatloaf

& laughed about something
that i really didn't find all that funny

*

one fox holds the door & they start to exit out
onto the sidewalk they're everywhere
stomach swollen   lips puckered sucking on straws
shoved in glasses of strawberry milkshakes
like it was a summer night stroll   1950s

the plates & forks are now gone   replaced by
boxing gloves that all have age to them
cracks filled with the peeled skin from chins of a
tougher generation

the smell of leather thick in the crowd
one spoke with the voice of my grandfather

said that in a white t-shirt
he's never look as cool as brando looks   but after
a sixer of pabst he really doesn't give a damn
because cool or not he's still just skin & bones
like every man   so that means a fair shot
at kicking his ass   & fair
is fair

                           *

a gun   someone shouted   A gun
a GUN   the words rang through the streets
all the fox eyes looked in many directions
i looked too

but never saw the gun before hearing the first shot

it all makes me wonder
can you feel moments   of danger
without anger

*

looking back   over the edge
there are still foxes on the street

twine in my hands turns to ivy & i drop it
watch it twist a few times
like a fish on a hook

lands in a sink full of dirty dishes

*

looking around
no longer on a roof   now in a different place
things look familiar   this apartment is very similar
to the layout of the trailer house that i lived in
the year that my first daughter was born

lora walks quickly into the kitchen

my god   it has been so long
since you have been close enough
for me to touch you
        she says

have you seen all the foxes outside

for some reason i can't talk
i just stare at lora's teeth

they're still just as white as they were when we met
in the ninth grade

*

i want to tell her that they're lovely
so i smile showing mine   & point at them
with my finger

she doesn't understand what i'm doing

she hugs me
& i'm concerned that she thinks i've gone crazy

i don't know
maybe i have

An Acquired Taste

reggie tells me
that when he was young
he saw a woman stick the head of a snake
into her mouth & moan
like she was having an orgasm

says that when he sees a snake in the grass

he thinks about her

& about how some things
are just really

fucked up

An Acquired Taste

Two Haiku

it's not a diamond
you're stoned
holding a dog's tooth up to the sun

in winter
a junkie that dies in an alley
won't rot until spring

Four to Six

the worst part wasn't when she left him
it was when she never returned

& he had kept all the items she had left behind
sealed in a box under his bed   said that
he thinks about it all the time   yet

it hadn't been opened in eight months   confessed
he had even saved a bedsheet that was stained with
faded blood spots from her menstrual cycle

after we finished a second cup of coffee

he asked me   if you rate on a scale from one to ten
how crazy do you think i am

Cheeking Haldol

she said their bodies stacked up
like snapped twigs in a ditch
dusted with the first frost
of '84

that saturday morning
daddy soaked the pile with kerosene
lit all seventeen dogs on fire
sang that kenny & dolly song
islands in the stream
as they burned

said some things
are not meant for a person to see
but i still see them

i used to see daddy's face
how it looked before
i pulled the trigger
but i don't see him much anymore

it's just the sight of those goddamn dogs

wet-tongued-spirits
licking me to sleep every night
in a corner

Pearl

eating a roast beef sandwich as she explains
how she wants to cut off a piece of her ear
& paint it the color of a pearl

so that she can toss it back into the sea
from high upon a rock cliff similar to one
her mother described to her as a little girl

i tell her   hope it all works out

listening to her talk   to her chew her meat & bread
to two cars pass by   to that voice inside me saying
how the pretty girls in this town all seem to be crazy

when she asks   if the roles were reversed
& that silly little bitch had died first
. . . do you think that romeo
would have said   O happy dagger

With Ten Toes & an Extra Heartbeat inside You

you throw out rib bones
like boomerangs
beyond veins
the slow rolling rivers
that all meet
at the mouth of a heart

there's something special
about captured moments like this

guiding my fingertips against your skin
i traverse the stretch marks
that have materialized
like constellations spread across
the pale night sky
we dream beneath

Four Flights to Freedom

on her first night we laugh
at the cabinet doors that are missing their knobs

as sounds from a gay bar enter through a broken window
& drag queens smoke cigarettes—

sharing gossip in the hallway
allison tells me she's excited to finally be living alone

a single air mattress
inflated on the floor of her bedroom

attempts to provide separation from the hardwood
as her tequila splashed lips blow kisses that travel

on the summer winds
whispering impending departure

the only ghost that she senses in the room
sings a sinatra tune
about love

& nothing seems scary tonight

Meth Rock in His Pocket

my heart like a bone
laid in a woven basket like bread
ribs aged almost forty years
i know my fate
the feeling of being ripped open
by an animal's tooth doesn't saddened me anymore

bentley though
his heart's like a handful of water
falling upon the parched lips of all that follow
sometimes i just watch him
he looks like a red-haired jesus christ spreading love
in a city park

last night he asked me about his mother again
said he wished she'd just come back to see him
& i didn't know what to say
because i've never told him the truth
that four years ago she disappeared
while chasing a man with a meth rock in his pocket
& that i never tried to stop her

because i knew better
than to wage a war that i'd never win

with all the demons she had inside of her

i would have had more success
lying on my back & trying to piss
on the side of the sun

On The Tip Of Our Tongues

*we, too, fell from above,
entered the earth's atmosphere,
and burned.*

—Heather Minette

My Best Friend
for reggie

live in a glass house
throw stones through the ceiling

swear they land like bombs
but don't detonate
just collect in the night sky
on ten squares chalked across a fantasy

now you say
every angel in heaven is a hopscotch champion

On a Thursday

i finished a ten-hour shift painting houses
under a sun in summer
stumbled home to a kitchen that still smelled
like last night's greasy supper
nothing new

really just wanting to sit down
shit & then drown in a bathtub of saltwater
she wanted to have sex
sitting shirtless in a chair

it's good for a relationship
she said
yeah   i replied
still being in love is too

she didn't say another word that evening

when i finally joined her in bed
i dreamt that all the dogs from hell
had suddenly fallen down on the sidewalks
& turned into piles of sand
store owners came outside to scoop them all up
& poured them into hourglasses

when i woke i had a strange feeling in my chest
wasn't sure what it was
rolling across the bed
i kissed her on the shoulder

three months later we called it quits

Reggie's Advice During My 1st Marriage

they're stupid
but even flies eventually give up on dead things

& move on

Continued Quest for a John Dorsey Book

reggie laughed out loud
& told me good luck

when i said

i'd pay a couple hundred dollars
for sodomy

Reunion

monday evening
reggie's daughters came to visit

it had been six years
since he had last seen them

when they arrived he greeted them
they didn't speak

he flicked his tongue out & in quickly
to try & break the silence

they never cracked a smile
or made eye contact

he looked back at me for advice
his eyes open glassy
desperation

i don't know
that i'd ever seen that side of him

like blood
after a bullet enters

small pieces of his toughness
dripped down his forehead
slowly

Forced Sober

days are getting rougher
miles growing greater
distance is the demon's chin i swing at

knockout punches in dreams
each time forget how it feels to fight
palm fist feet elbow knuckles blood
brow skin eyes lips bruised

i'm always tougher in dreams
excess muscles mind skill luck
lately they've all failed me
finished in first rounds

when i wake early i feel beaten
sore back arms legs wrists hips
standing naked in a kitchen
waiting on coffee to brew
black donut shop 12 ounce cup

sip swallow sip again
recall fragments of dream fights
i never fully remember them all
it's probably for the best

looking out the window
i tell the fading moon it's irritating
you're a whisky bottle
& it has now been two months
since i last put my hands on your curves

Kiss & Tell

reggie tells a story about a girl
he knew for two weeks
at a petco
says they got real close
one night she stuck her tongue deep into his mouth
swirled it softly
& his legs got weak

i tell him about thursday night at the villa
how my lips against yours
made my body feel like a sun rising
above a city
your exhale becoming my inhale
warmth expanded & alive again

he says bullshit
says he doesn't believe that
i had actually kissed you

& that's okay

i tell him that
i don't believe his story either

That Taste on the Tip of Our Tongues

a cooking show said salmon croquettes
reggie asked
what the hell are salmon croquettes
my childhood dinnertime memory
i replied   i hated them
would sit in defiance until given options
eat it   go hungry
would choose go hungry
& slip out the back door on 7th street
a vacant lot had plenty of red clover
i would chew & suck the sweetness
out of the flowers
thinking to myself
fuck salmon croquettes
fuck options
i was winning the battle until winter
then i thought to myself
fuck winter
i was hungry

reggie said when he was young
he ate a cockroach
on a dare from his father
said it was one of the last times
he ever saw him alive

the mood turned melancholy

i switched the channel to californication
charlie was eating out a girl
that was a squirter
reggie said   yes sir

& i could see in his smile
that he had memories of ex-girlfriends
flooding his mind now too

they were all falling quick & hard

like rain

coming down sideways

Hot Action & Appreciation

you never know if they've a heart like cotton candy
or an accelerant waiting
in a molly bottle with the wick lit

he says   yeah yeah
then tells me he has been thinking
about reciting love words to the next one
that lights a fire inside of him

asks what i think about this

. . . one raindrop drips & splits into two
two drops now drip from moistened lips
so make requests   your hips   your chest
where should this wet passion be placed . . .

that's a good question   i tell him
i've got one that's constantly on my mind

. . . how to make time stand still
truth is i really don't have
the definitive answer for the world
all i have is the nights
sleeping beside you on that couch . . .

he listens   says he likes it
might steal it
whisper it into a woman's ear

& my only hope for him is that she whispers back

What Am I Going To Do With My Life

reggie suggests i write a graphic novel
real smutty with black & white drawings

he can't read a single word though
i can't draw either   a horrible idea

he says the opening chapter should
be about that one month back in 2008
when he banged several different ladies

isn't that something   he banged several
in one month during a stretch when i hadn't gotten
a single piece of action in almost three

that sounds like a terrible opening

you're just jealous
because i was riding the lightning shotgun
like shooting stars with sunglow albinos pretending
they were all jennifer aniston while you sat at the
kitchen table exhaling desperation like it was
marlboro smoke from your lips
he says
& your wife was just as miserable as you

some days   he's a real fucking prick

& i ask myself

how can you argue with the truth though

Nuclear Goodbyes

it's all in your tone
but that's not how you argue anymore
my children tell me
emotions in the waves of voices
have been lost in the leaps
& the bounds of convenience
it's all uppercase letters on a screen now
followed by exclamation points
to make the point
attach an emoji that is crying one tear
angry face
shades of all your frustration
attach another one crying two tears
followed by blue hearts
then red ones
that are broken in two pieces
i shake my head
because what they say is truth
i too have spoken from the gut
without saying a word
i ask my children
how their children's children
will argue with the ones they love
when those rough days
in their futures start to arrive

& they have no clue
i have no clue
guess time will tell
if they will even be given
the opportunity to quarrel

because today
there are still men building bombs
to drop from the sky
on human beings

& that is sadder
than anything i've just said

Traveler
for annie menebroker

you said you had an inconsistent fear of being lost
yet you knew that one road leads there

compass needles point towards magnetic love

please borrow a burning star from the sky
to hang like a wreath from your front door
when you see our silhouettes

because   annie

we're all coming down that one road now
to visit you

When not traveling on highways across America, Victor Clevenger spends his days in a Madhouse and his nights writing poetry. He lives with his second ex-wife, and together they raise six children in a small town northeast of Kansas City, MO. Selected pieces of his work have appeared in print magazines and journals around the world, as well as at a variety of places online. His work has been nominated for the Best of the Net Anthology, as well as the Pushcart Prize. Victor is the author of several collections of poetry including *Sandpaper Lovin'* (Crisis Chronicles Press, 2017), *Congenital Pipe Dreams* (Spartan Press, 2017) and *A Finger in the Hornets' Nest* (Red Flag Poetry, 2018). He can be reached at: facebook.com/thepoetvictorclevenger

Poetry from the third turnbuckle!

More titles from Luchador Press:

Standing at the Intersection of Critical Mass and Event Horizon / Jason Ryberg

Sick / Daniel Crocker and John Dorsey

Corned Beef Hash by Candlelight / Victor Clevenger

CPSIA information can be obtained
at www.ICGtesting.com
Printed in the USA
FSHW012344070719
59775FS